Esperanza Rising

Grades 4-6

Written by Nat Reed
Illustrated by Ric Ward

ISBN 1-55035-771-9
Copyright 2005
Revised January 2006
All Rights Reserved * Printed in Canada

Permission to Reproduce

Permission is granted to the individual teacher who purchases one copy of this book to reproduce the student activity material for use in his/her classroom only. Reproduction of these materials for an entire school or for a school system, or for other colleagues or for commercial sale is <u>strictly prohibited</u>. No part of this publication may be transmitted in any form or by any means, electronic, mechanical, recording or otherwise without the prior written permission of the publisher. "We acknowledge the financial support of the Government of Canada through the Book Publishing Industry Development Program (BPIDP) for this project."

Published in the United States by:
On the Mark Press
3909 Witmer Road PMB 175
Niagara Falls, New York
14305
www.onthemarkpress.com

Published in Canada by:
S&S Learning Materials
15 Dairy Avenue
Napanee, Ontario
K7R 1M4
www.sslearning.com

At A Glance

Learning Expectations	Ch 1	Ch 2	Ch 3	Ch 4	Ch 5	Ch 6	Ch 7	Ch 8	Ch 9	Ch 10	Ch 11	Ch 12	Ch 13
Reading Comprehension													
• Identify and describe story elements	•	•	•	•	•	•	•	•	•	•	•	•	•
• Summarize events/details	•				•								•
Reasoning & Critical Thinking													
• Character traits, comparisons		•		•	•		•	•				•	•
• Use context cues - identify analogies					•					•			•
• Make inferences (i.e., why events occurred, characters' thoughts and feelings, etc.)	•			•	•	•	•						
• Determine the meaning of colloquialisms and other phrases					•			•	•	•			•
• Understand abstract concepts					•		•	•				•	•
• Develop opinions and personal interpretations		•	•	•		•	•	•	•		•	•	•
• Write a letter, newspaper editorial						•				•			
• Conduct an interview									•				
• Develop research skills	•	•			•		•			•			
• Create a poster, book cover											•		•
• Identify conflict								•					
• Create a timeline													•
• Identify foreshadowing	•												
• Identify a cliffhanger	•											•	
Vocabulary Development, Grammar & Word Use													
• Synonyms, antonyms and homonyms										•	•		•
• Similes	•												
• Syllables			•										
• Compound Words												•	
• Descriptive words and phrases		•	•										
• Parts of speech									•	•			
• Dictionary and thesaurus skills	•	•	•	•				•				•	
• Use words correctly in sentences	•		•		•	•	•						
• Alphabetical order					•								
• Singular/plural nouns				•									
• Root words										•			
• Using capitals, correct punctuation					•								

Esperanza Rising
by Pam Muñoz Ryan

Table of Contents

At A Glance™ 2

Overall Expectations 4

List of Skills 5

Teacher Suggestions 6

Synopsis 7

Author Biography 8

Student Checklist 9

Reproducible Student Booklet 10

Answer Key 61

Esperanza Rising
by Pam Muñoz Ryan

Overall Expectations

The students will:

- develop their skills in reading, writing, listening and oral communication

- use good literature as a vehicle for developing skills required by curriculum expectations: reasoning and critical thinking, knowledge of language structure, vocabulary building, and use of conventions

- become meaningfully engaged in the drama of literature through a variety of types of questions and activities

- identify and describe elements of stories (i.e., plot, main idea, characters, setting)

- learn and review many skills in order to develop good reading habits

- provide clear answers to questions and well-constructed explanations

- organize and classify information to clarify thinking

- learn about the destructive nature of societal prejudice and stereotyping

- relate events and feelings found in the novel to their own lives and experiences

- appreciate the importance of friendship and loyalty in personal relationships

- appreciate that the growth of one's character is more important than wealth or social status

- learn the importance of dealing with adversity and developing perseverance in the face of adversity

- state their own interpretation of a written work, using evidence from the work and from their own knowledge and experience

Esperanza Rising
by Pam Muñoz Ryan

List of Skills

Vocabulary Development

1. Identifying/creating similes
2. Locating descriptive words/phrases
3. Listing synonyms and antonyms
4. Using capitals and punctuation
5. Identifying syllables
6. Listing compound words
7. Using singular/plural nouns
8. Using content cues: analogies
9. Identifying parts of speech
10. Determining alphabetical order
11. Determining meaning of Spanish words
12. Identification of root words

Setting Activities

1. Summarize the details of a setting
2. Identify hardships of moving to a new home
3. Create a time chart

Plot Activities

1. Complete a timeline of events
2. Identify foreshadowing
3. Determine the role of others in one's personal growth
4. Identify conflict in the story
5. Identify cliffhangers

Character Activities

1. Determine character traits
2. Compare two characters
3. Understand concepts such as *perseverance, self-respect, stereotypes*
4. Relating personal experiences

Creative and Critical Thinking

1. Research different fruits/vegetables
2. Write an editorial on an issue
3. Write a letter to a friend
4. Conduct an interview
5. Identify poetic images
6. Write a description of personal feelings

Art Activities

1. Design a poster
2. Design a cover for the novel

 # Esperanza Rising
by Pam Muñoz Ryan

Teacher Suggestions

This resource may be used in a variety of ways:

1. The student booklet focuses on one chapter of the novel at a time. Each of these sections contains the following activities:

   a) **Before you read the chapter** (reasoning and critical thinking skills)
   b) **Vocabulary building** (dictionary and thesaurus skills)
   c) **Questions on the chapter** (reading comprehension skills)
   d) **Language activities** (grammar, punctuation, word structure and extension activities)

2. Students may read the novel at their own speed and then select, or be assigned, a variety of questions and activities.

3. **Bulletin Board and Interest Center Ideas**: Themes might include Mexico, California, fruit/vegetable farming, the Great Depression.

4. **Pre-Reading Activities**: *Esperanza Rising* may also be used in conjunction with themes of self-esteem, perseverance, family values, societal prejudice (the poor, immigrants), the danger of placing too much emphasis on social status, and losing a parent.

5. **Independent Reading Approach**: Students who are able to work independently may attempt to complete the assignments in a self-directed manner. Initially these students should participate in the pre-reading activities with the rest of the class. Students should familiarize themselves with the reproducible student booklet. Completed work sheets should be submitted so that the teacher may note how quickly and accurately the students are working. Students may be brought together periodically to discuss issues in specific sections of the novel.

6. **Fine Art Activities**: Students may integrate such topics as Mexico and California, farm crops (especially fruits), modes of transportation in the 1930s (i.e., trains, wagons) and an introduction to the fundamentals of crocheting.

7. Encourage the students to keep a reading log in which they record their readings each day and their thoughts about the passage.

8. Students should keep all their work together in one place. A portfolio cover is provided for this purpose (see p. 10).

9. Students should not be expected to complete all activities. Teachers should allow choice, and in some cases, match the activity to the student's ability.

10. Students should keep track (in their portfolio) of the activities they complete.

Esperanza Rising
by Pam Muñoz Ryan

Synopsis

The main character of *Esperanza Rising* is a young Mexican girl named Esperanza Ortega. She is a smart, pampered young girl from a rich family, yet lacks even the simplest skills (cooking, cleaning, etc.).

Esperanza lives in Aguascalientes, Mexico with her mother and father on *El Rancho de las Rosas*. Her father is a wealthy plantation owner who employs several dozen workers. Esperanza attends a private school while still being friends with the children of her father's ranch hands, including Miguel.

The day before Esperanza's birthday, her father is killed by bandits. With her Papa dead, the house and land become the property of Esperanza's uncle, Luis. Luis offers to buy the house from Esperanza's mother, but she refuses. He then offers his hand in marriage, but is again refused, for Esperanza's mother knows that Luis is a cruel, evil man. Luis then sets fire to the grapevines and then their house.

Esperanza and her mother escape Mexico with Miguel and his family and travel to California to work in the fields. Esperanza quickly discovers that she must become stronger and more useful, learning to sweep, cook, take care of children, and work in the fields. Her problems are compounded when her mother becomes seriously ill.

With increased responsibilities, Esperanza grows more confident and self-reliant. Finally, with the help of Miguel and his supportive family, Esperanza and her mother are able to overcome all of the tremendous odds they have encountered and begin to feel that there is hope for the future in their new home and country.

Esperanza Rising
by Pam Muñoz Ryan

Author Biography

Pam Muñoz Ryan

Pam Muñoz Ryan has written over 25 books for young people including *Esperanza Rising*, winner of the Pura Belpré Medal. Her picture books include the award-winning *Amelia and Eleanor Go for a Ride* and *When Marian Sang*. She received her Bachelor's and Master's Degrees at San Diego State University and now lives in north San Diego County with her husband and four children.

Pam Muñoz Ryan was born and raised in California's San Joaquin Valley. She grew up as a part of a large extended family and considers herself truly American because of her cultural background. She is Spanish, Mexican, Basque, Italian, and Oklahoman.

As a young girl Pam spent many long, hot Californian summers hanging out at the local air-conditioned library, where she got hooked on reading books. She knew from then on that she wanted to spend her life around books and went on to become a teacher. At the encouragement of a friend who thought she could write, she began her first book. That's when she finally knew what she really wanted to do.

Esperanza Rising
by Pam Muñoz Ryan

Student Checklist

Name: _____

Assignment	Grade/Level	Comments

Esperanza Rising
by Pam Muñoz Ryan

Name: _____

Esperanza Rising
by Pam Muñoz Ryan

Chapter One

Las Uvas - Grapes

Before you read the chapter:

Mexico and its people form an important part of this novel. Investigate this remarkable country and record three interesting facts about it. Then get together with a group of three other students and share your facts.

_____
_____
_____

Esperanza Rising is set in 1930. List four things that would be different about living during the 1930's compared to now.

_____
_____
_____

Vocabulary:

Choose a word from the list to complete each sentence.

magnified	congregate	anticipation	premonition
philosophical	precisely	resurrected	tormented
propriety	resentment	distinguished	forlorn

1. Esperanza was looking forward to her father's return with great _____.

2. She had an awful _____ that something was wrong.

3. The little girl was very _____ when her puppy disappeared.

4. A feeling of guilt _____ the prisoner.

Esperanza Rising
by Pam Muñoz Ryan

5. Esperanza's mother tried to be very _____ about their problems.

6. The crowd of farmers began to _____ in front of the old barn.

7. The insect was _____ under the microscope.

8. The boy's aunt left _____ at eight o'clock.

9. The people felt a lot of _____ toward the country's cruel president.

10. Christians believe that Jesus Christ was _____ from the grave.

11. Esperanza's grandmother was an unusual, _____ woman.

12. Señora Ortega was a very dignified woman with a fine sense of _____.

Questions

1. What crop was being harvested at El Rancho de las Rosas in this chapter?
   _____
   _____

2. What is the setting of the story as this chapter opens? Remember your answer should include both time and place.
   _____
   _____

3. Which three friends were coming to Esperanza's party?
   _____
   _____

4. What had taken place ten years earlier in Mexico that still made the large landowners nervous? How did Esperanza's father treat the local peasants?
   _____
   _____

Esperanza Rising
by Pam Muñoz Ryan

5. What pastime did Abuelita enjoy? What did Esperanza suggest it took her mind off?
   _____
   _____

6. Why was Abuelita crocheting the blanket?
   _____
   _____

7. Where did Alfonso always talk about going?
   _____
   _____

8. What did Esperanza mean when she told Miguel that a deep river ran between them?
   _____
   _____

9. What important job did Tío Marco have? What was Esperanza's impression of him?
   _____
   _____

10. Who did Hortensia say would find Esperanza's father?
    _____
    _____

11. What terrible news did Esperanza receive at the end of the chapter?
    _____
    _____

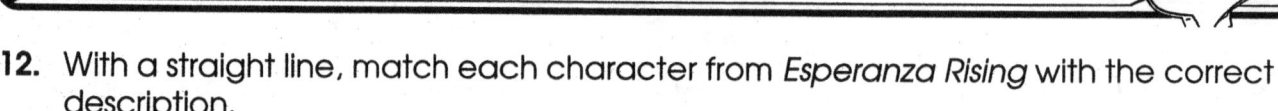
Esperanza Rising
by Pam Muñoz Ryan

12. With a straight line, match each character from *Esperanza Rising* with the correct description.

    a) Hortensia   Esperanza's father

    b) Abuelita   *El jefe* (the boss)

    c) Marisol Rodríguez   Papa's stepbrother

    d) Ramona Ortega   Esperanza's best friend

    e) Sixto Ortega   Esperanza's grandmother

    f) Alfonso   Hortensia's son

    g) Miguel   Esperanza's mother

    h) Tío Luis   The housekeeper

Language Activities

1. The author seems to enjoy using **similes** to describe different things. (A **simile** is a comparison using the words **like** or **as**.) Examples from this chapter include:

    "... the tool was edged like a razor."
    "The short blade was curved like a scythe."

    Use similes to compare the following:

    The howl of the cold north wind - _____

    The cry of a hungry baby - _____

    The dark of a moonless night - _____

Esperanza Rising
by Pam Muñoz Ryan

2. This novel has many **Spanish** words throughout. Usually the author indicates the English meaning next to the Spanish word. For each of the following Spanish words from this chapter, find out its English meaning from the story and place it beside its Spanish equivalent.

Spanish Word	English Meaning
campesinos	
reina	
tío	
la cosecha	
El Rancho de las Rosas	
Cuídate los dedos	

3. **Foreshadowing** is defined as *to suggest beforehand*. This chapter contains at least three examples of foreshadowing. For example, on page eleven Esperanza says, "Mama, the neighbors warned him just last night about the bandits." Here we are introduced to the idea that her father's life might be endangered because of the bandits. See if you can find at least one of the other two examples of this literary device. A bonus if you find both!

_____
_____
_____
_____
_____
_____

Esperanza Rising
by Pam Muñoz Ryan

Chapter Two

Las Papayas - Papayas

Before you read the chapter:

You have probably noticed that all of the chapters in this novel are named after fruits. **Papaya** is a fruit that is not as well known as many others. Research this fruit and tell at least three interesting facts about its appearance, taste, where it grows, or any other facts you might uncover.

_____
_____

Vocabulary:

Using the words from this chapter, complete the following crossword puzzle.

anguish	ambush	overwhelm	attentive	stroke	higo
offend	batiste	wistful	custom	awkward	solution
lime	propose	throttle	intend	reality	Anza
Luis	papaya	patio	joy	adapt	rosehip
Ramona					

Down
1. A fabric made from fibres
2. The act of striking
4. Hurt the feelings of someone
6. A fruit
8. Strangle or choke
10. Too much to do
12. Get used to something
13. Esperanza's nickname
14. A green fruit
16. Lie in wait for
17. Esperanza's mother
18. Esperanza's uncle
19. Fruit featured in title of next chapter

Across
3. Happy
5. Hurt; pain
6. A paved outdoor area
7. A longing feeling
9. Suggest
11. Realness
15. Ungraceful
16. Thoughtful
17. Fruit of the rose plant
20. Answer
21. Mean to
22. Habit

Esperanza Rising
by Pam Muñoz Ryan

Questions

1. What shocking news did Esperanza tell Señor Rodríguez?

   _____
   _____

2. Why did Esperanza finally open her birthday gifts?

   _____
   _____

3. What was the last gift her father gave to her?

   _____
   _____

Esperanza Rising
by Pam Muñoz Ryan

4. Why did Esperanza's uncle come to the ranch every day?
   _____
   _____

5. Why do you think it was so upsetting for Esperanza to see her uncle wearing her father's belt buckle?
   _____
   _____

6. Why did Tío Luis' offer to buy the ranch house upset Esperanza's mother?
   _____
   _____

7. What proposal did Luis make to Esperanza's mother? Why did Luis want this? Why do you think this proposal offended her?
   _____
   _____
   _____

8. What did Abuelita say the rosehip contained?
   _____
   _____

9. What name did Miguel call Esperanza?
   _____
   _____

10. What rumor had Miguel heard in town?
    _____
    _____

 # Esperanza Rising
by Pam Muñoz Ryan

Language Activity

The author, **Pam Muñoz Ryan**, is an excellent writer who includes many **poetic images** in this novel. One expression in this chapter is very poetic: "the echoes of their footsteps deepened their sadness."

What specific **sights** or **sounds** have caused you to feel sad in the past? Think of two or three examples and explain why this happened.

_____
_____
_____
_____
_____
_____
_____
_____
_____
_____
_____
_____
_____

Esperanza Rising
by Pam Muñoz Ryan

Chapter Three

Los Higos - Figs

Before you read the chapter:

Losing your home to a fire would probably be one of the worst things that could ever happen to someone. What are a few important personal possessions a person might lose if his or her home was destroyed by fire?

_____
_____

Vocabulary:

In each of the following sets of words, **underline** the one word which does not belong. Then write a sentence explaining why it does not fit.

1. enormous   gigantic   famished   huge
   _____

2. delight   wail   whine   whimper
   _____

3. donate   give   purchase   bestow
   _____

4. option   devotion   selection   choice
   _____

5. fierce   savage   ferocious   affluent
   _____

Esperanza Rising
by Pam Muñoz Ryan

6. resentful   bitter   acrimonious   persuaded

_____

7. accidental   purposeful   intentional   deliberate

_____

Questions

Cloze Call

Complete the following exercise filling in the correct words from the word box.

sadness	ashes	phoenix	convent	visa
influence	nuns	Luis	uncles	figs
Miguel	servants	United States	proposal	grapes
poverty	Abuelita	home		

A huge fire destroyed Esperanza's _____. _____, though, was able to save Abuelita from the fire. Everyone knew that the _____ had arranged for the fire to be set.

Tío Luis told them that Esperanza and her mother could live with the _____ as long as another tragedy didn't happen. Mama said she would consider Luis' _____.

There would be no income on the ranch that season because there were no _____. If Mama moved to another part of Mexico, she would live in _____ because Luis' _____ was far-reaching.

Esperanza Rising
by Pam Muñoz Ryan

Esperanza and her mother decided to go with Hortensia's family to the _____. _____ planned on joining Esperanza and the others later, when she was stronger. Abuelita's sisters were _____ and would get duplicates of Mama's _____. Mama's leaving would be a great insult to _____.

Abuelita told Esperanza the story of a young bird, the _____, who was reborn from its own _____.

Esperanza and her mother were given clothing from the poor box at the _____.

Señor Rodríguez always carried a basket of _____ to his meetings with Esperanza's mother and the others.

When Esperanza left her home for the last time she was filled with _____.

Esperanza Rising
by Pam Muñoz Ryan

Language Activities

1. The author describes the results of the fire as follows:

   "It looked as if someone had taken a giant comb, dipped it in black paint, and gently swirled it across a huge canvas."

   Think of another way of **describing** the results of a fire - with what might you compare such a tragedy?

   _____
   _____
   _____
   _____
   _____

2. Choose **ten** words from chapter three with two or more **syllables**. Indicate the syllables by drawing a line between each syllable.

   ### Example: pork/chop

Esperanza Rising
by Pam Muñoz Ryan

Chapter Four

Las Guayabas - Guavas

Before you read the chapter:

Tell what you think the following statements mean, and give **your impression** of each of them:

"The rich take care of the rich and the poor take care of those who have less than they have."

_____
_____

"Those with Spanish blood, who have the fairest complexions in the land, are the wealthiest."

_____
_____

Vocabulary:

Draw a straight line to connect the vocabulary word to its definition. Remember to use a straight edge (like a ruler).

1.	renegade	constant
2.	persistent	suitcase
3.	mesmerize	reddish brown
4.	exotic	spellbind
5.	frail	rise and fall
6.	undulate	familiar
7.	valise	boring
8.	monotonous	rebel
9.	russet	delicate
10.	intimate	strange

Esperanza Rising
by Pam Muñoz Ryan

Questions

1. Describe how Mama, Esperanza and Hortensia escaped to Zacatecas.

2. a) What incident did Hortensia remind Esperanza of on the wagon ride?

   b) What did Miguel do to save them?

   c) What did Miguel ask for as a reward?

3. How long did it take for them to get to Zacatecas?

4. What did Esperanza find so disturbing about the people in the railway car?

5. a) Describe how Esperanza upset the little girl in the railway car.

Esperanza Rising
by Pam Muñoz Ryan

b) What did Esperanza's mother give the little girl to make her feel better?

_____
_____

6. Why did Esperanza's mother think it was all right to tell the "egg woman" their problems?

_____
_____

Language Activities

1. Esperanza feels a real sense of **claustrophobia** when she is in the wagon. Have you ever experienced such a powerful fear as this? Describe this experience. Make sure you describe how you **felt** during your ordeal.

_____
_____

2. Write the **plural** of the following nouns from this chapter. Be careful - you may wish to consult a dictionary for some of these words.

Singular Noun	Plural Noun
wagon	
dress	
cactus	
valise	
child	
belly	
complexion	
eyebrow	
railroad	
baby	

Esperanza Rising
by Pam Muñoz Ryan

3. Match each of the following **Spanish** words with the correct **English** meaning:

a) *ratón*   lever

b) *carpetas*   good luck

c) *gracias*   you're welcome

d) *de nada*   sweets

e) *dulces*   thank you

f) *palanca*   lace doilies

g) *buena suerta*   rat

Esperanza Rising
by Pam Muñoz Ryan

Chapter Five

Los Melones - Cantaloupes

Before you read the chapter:

Think about a time when you traveled to a new place (a different city, country or even a new school). Describe your **feelings** when you first arrived at this location. Why do you think you felt this way?

_____
_____

Did you know that the **cantaloupe** is a member of the melon family? Cantaloupe is named for the town of Cantalupo near Rome. In Europe they are called musk melons. Research three other interesting facts about the cantaloupe and share them with a classmate.

_____
_____
_____

Vocabulary:

Choose a word from the list that means the **same** or **nearly the same** as the underlined word.

tied	departed	irritated	thin	motionless
ill	feeling	purposefully	appearance	flowed

1. Esperanza and her family **disembarked** from the station. _____

2. The dirty pool of water was **stagnant**. _____

3. The **demeanor** of the policeman grew very angry. _____

4. Esperanza became extremely **agitated** by Marta. _____

Esperanza Rising
by Pam Muñoz Ryan

5. The vegetation in desert lands is **sparse**. _____

6. The truck ride made her feel **nauseous**. _____

7. The small dog was **tethered** to the porch. _____

8. Esperanza enjoyed the **sensation** of flying. _____

9. Her tears **cascaded** down her cheeks. _____

10. Mama **deliberately** told the man the truth. _____

Questions

1. How did Mama's change in demeanor effect the immigration official?
   _____
   _____

2. What happened at the border to those who had no proof of work?
   _____
   _____

3. Why did Miguel and Alfonso almost miss the train at the border?
   _____
   _____

4. How had Joan and Josefina come to know about Esperanza and her family?
   _____
   _____

5. According to Isabel, what was so hard about living in El Centro?
   _____
   _____

Esperanza Rising
by Pam Muñoz Ryan

6. a) What did Esperanza's father tell her that she would hear if she lay on the land and was very still and quiet?

   _____
   _____

   b) Describe the result of Esperanza's first attempt.

   _____
   _____

7. Describe how Marta treated Esperanza.

   _____
   _____

8. Why did the landowners keep the different groups of people apart?

   _____
   _____

9. What did Marta suggest be done to obtain better working and living conditions?

   _____
   _____

 # Esperanza Rising
by Pam Muñoz Ryan

Language Activities

1. Esperanza came across to many people as being rather snobbish. In this chapter Marta asks her, "So you're a princess who's come to be a peasant? Where's all your finery?" Describe a time in your life when you encountered someone with a stuck-up attitude like Esperanza. What did it make you feel like to be treated this way? Do you think you have ever treated anyone else like this -- perhaps without meaning to?

_____
_____
_____
_____
_____
_____

2. Place the following words from this chapter in **alphabetical order**.

| plants | paws | piled | Oklahoma | papers |
| officials | package | property | past | private |

_____   _____
_____   _____
_____   _____
_____   _____
_____   _____

Esperanza Rising
by Pam Muñoz Ryan

Chapter Six

Las Cebollas - Onions

Before you read the chapter:

Drawing on your own experiences or from what you have heard or read, list a couple of things which **would** be fun about **camping in the wilderness** and then list a couple of things that **would not** be much fun.

___
___
___

Vocabulary:

Solve the word search using the words from the word box. Remember - the words may be horizontal, vertical or diagonal. They may be forward or even backward!

Marta	Juan	Esperanza	bestow	anticipate
platform	hesitate	fiesta	peasant	accost
wrung	transfer	somberly	retrieve	relent
humiliation	perspiration	Mama	frustrating	mechanic

```
A R E L E N T A S D F E R T A
Z P E R S P I R A T I O N R N
N Y U T T R A N S F E R F G T
A A A Y U R I O T N A S A E P I
R M C A S I F G H J T K L L C
E Z A C C H E S I T A T E A I
P X A R O V B V N M E R T T P
S L M J T S H B E S T O W F A
E D A S A A T G J U A N R O T
H U M I L I A T I O N V U R E
X C V B C I N A H C E M N N K
D Y L R E B M O S F G H G J K
F R U S T R A T I N G D F S G
```

Esperanza Rising
by Pam Muñoz Ryan

Questions

1. What was Esperanza's first impression of her new home?

2. According to Mama, what **two** choices did Esperanza now have?

3. a) Why did Esperanza believe she was still rich?

   b) Give your opinion on this point of view.

4. What job was Esperanza assigned while her mother and the others went off to work?

5. What drastic change had Mama made to her appearance?

6. Why **didn't** Esperanza pull her hand away from Silva?

Esperanza Rising
by Pam Muñoz Ryan

7. Why did Melina think that Esperanza might know her husband?
   _____
   _____

8. Describe **four** of the steps Isabel took when washing a diaper.
   _____
   _____
   _____
   _____

9. Why did Esperanza not know how to change a diaper or sweep a floor?
   _____
   _____

10. What is ironic about Miguel's statement to Esperanza: "Someday, you might make a very good servant."
    _____
    _____

Esperanza Rising
by Pam Muñoz Ryan

Language Activities

1. A lot has happened to Esperanza since her father was killed and she had to leave her home in Aguascalientes, Mexico. With a partner **make a list** of the most important adventures that Esperanza has endured during this short time. Then using this list, pretend that you are Esperanza and **write a letter** to her best friend, Marisol Rodríguez, back home. Be sure to tell Marisol about the exiting things that have happened to you and describe your feelings throughout this time.

2. Rewrite the following sentences putting in the correct **capitalization** and **punctuation**.

    a) esperanza rode the train to los angeles

    b) señor rodríguez enjoyed picking peaches guavas onions and plums in california

    c) from zacatecas isabel drove a wagon to san francisco

# Esperanza Rising
*by Pam Muñoz Ryan*

Chapter Seven

Las Almendras - Almonds

Before you read the chapter:

Did you know that **almonds** are the number one ranked nut crop in the United States, and that there are approximately 10,000 almond orchards in California alone? Research **three** interesting facts about the almond. You may wish to include the varieties grown in California, and where else in the world they are grown. You may even wish to include a recipe that includes almonds.

_____
_____
_____

Mexico is famous for its delicious foods. Choose one of the following **Mexican specialties** and describe how it is made and what ingredients it might contain: **tortilla, taco, enchilada, nachos, chili**.

_____
_____
_____

Vocabulary:

Write a sentence using the following words. Make sure that the meaning of the word is clear in your sentence.

taunting - _____
_____

specialty - _____
_____

Esperanza Rising
by Pam Muñoz Ryan

migrant - _____
_____

accustomed - _____
_____

extravagant - _____
_____

Questions

1. What does Esperanza mean when she says that the "bruises had been to her pride"?
   _____
   _____

2. a) Describe what Miguel and Alfonso made for Esperanza and her mother.
   _____
   _____

   b) Why do you think the boys went to all that trouble when Esperanza acted like such a snob?
   _____
   _____

3. What did Mama mean by saying that "Papa's heart would find us wherever we go"?
   _____
   _____

Esperanza Rising
by Pam Muñoz Ryan

4. Why was Saturday evening so exciting in the camp?
   _____
   _____

5. What strategy did Isabel suggest was the best way to get over an embarrassment?
   _____
   _____

6. a) What did Marta urge the people to do at the peak of the cotton season?
   _____
   _____

   b) What were the **two** things they were fighting for?
   _____
   _____

7. Why wouldn't many of the people follow Marta's advice?
   _____
   _____

8. After hearing Marta speak, how did Esperanza feel when she talked about her former life in Aguascalientes?
   _____
   _____

 # Esperanza Rising
by Pam Muñoz Ryan

Language Activities

1. Why do you think that Esperanza "could be in the middle of so many people and still feel so alone"? What factors contributed to this feeling in her?
   _____
   _____
   _____

2. **Conflict** is an important element in a novel. There are generally three types of conflict: **person against person**; **person against self**; and **person against nature**. Find three examples of conflict in *Esperanza Rising*, and tell which type of conflict each is.

   a) _____
   _____
   _____
   _____

   b) _____
   _____
   _____
   _____

   c) _____
   _____
   _____
   _____

Esperanza Rising
by Pam Muñoz Ryan

Chapter Eight

Las Ciruelas - Plums

Before you read the chapter:

What do you think is the **most difficult** thing about looking after small children? What does a responsible baby-sitter have to be especially careful to watch for?
_____
_____

Vocabulary:

Choose a word from the list to complete each definition.

sympathetic	occasionally	preoccupied	peculiar	atrocious
spasm	frantic	grim	reposition	infection

1. To shift the place of an object is to _____ it.

2. Something unspeakably awful is said to be _____.

3. If something happens once in a while, it is said to happen _____.

4. When someone's thoughts are far away, they are said to be _____.

5. An extremely agitated person is often _____.

6. A _____ man is a person who is unusual.

7. Someone who lends a listening ear is often _____ to your concerns.

8. A _____ is an involuntary muscle contraction.

9. A person who looks very serious is said to be _____.

10. A sick person might have an _____.

 # Esperanza Rising
by Pam Muñoz Ryan

Questions

1. What caused Esperanza to worry about the babies?

2. What did she give the babies as a possible remedy?

3. According to Isabel, what had caused the babies' sickness?

4. What did Lupe often do that caused Esperanza some frantic moments?

5. According to Irene, what did both strikers and non-strikers want?

6. What terrifying thing happened during Irene's visit?

7. Why weren't Mama and the others rescued by the trucks?

Esperanza Rising
by Pam Muñoz Ryan

8. What prevented the strike?
   _____
   _____

9. Why will the strikers not have jobs tomorrow?
   _____
   _____

10. Why would Mama and the others have jobs the next day?
    _____
    _____

11. How did Mama change after the storm?
    _____
    _____

12. What is "Valley Fever"?
    _____
    _____

Esperanza Rising
by Pam Muñoz Ryan

Language Activity

Choose any **two characters** you have already met in this novel. **Compare** four things about these two people. Consider such things as physical appearance, personality, age, talents, attitude, etc.

Character One _____	Character Two _____
1.	
2.	
3.	
4.	

# Esperanza Rising
by Pam Muñoz Ryan

Chapter Nine

Las Papas - Potatoes

Before you read the chapter:

Tell about a time when you or a friend or family member was very sick. Describe how you felt (both physically and emotionally) and what was done to make you feel better.

_____
_____
_____

Vocabulary:

Synonyms are words with similar meanings. Using the context of the sentences below, choose the best synonym for the underlined word in each sentence.

1. Charlie was a very **nimble** gymnast.

    a) light   b) pleasant   c) untalented   d) agile

2. The **penetrating** north wind chilled them to the bone.

    a) piercing   b) confusing   c) invisible   d) frustrating

3. The inside of the shed was **cavernous**.

    a) empty   b) huge   c) old-fashioned   d) dumpy

4. Mama had a lot of **sympathy** for the peasants.

    a) advice   b) porridge   c) pity   d) education

Esperanza Rising
by Pam Muñoz Ryan

5. Esperanza **yearned** for her home back in Mexico.

   a) longed   b) prayed   c) called   d) played

6. Her attention was **riveted** on the coat.

   a) glancing   b) distracted c) swinging   d) fastened

7. Although it was California, the weather was **frigid**.

   a) windy   b) warm   c) cold   d) blustery

8. The Mexican **supervisor** took their names.

   a) administrator   b) farmer   c) planter   d) driver

Questions

1. What did Alfonso and Juan do to try to keep the cabin warmer?
   _____
   _____

2. What did Mama ask be brought to her from the valise when she was so sick?
   _____
   _____

3. Whom did Mama really need in her illness?
   _____
   _____

4. What does this expression mean: "This valley of Mama being sick?"
   _____
   _____

Esperanza Rising
by Pam Muñoz Ryan

5. What project did Esperanza take up to pass the time?

6. What was at the root of Mama's slow road to recovery?

7. Why did Esperanza feel that she needed to start a paying job?

8. If Esperanza was found to be a good worker at one job, what would probably happen?

9. What is done with the eye pieces from potatoes?

10. What is "repatriation"?

11. What three things did Esperanza say she wanted for Christmas?

12. What Christmas gift did Esperanza give to Mama?

Esperanza Rising
by Pam Muñoz Ryan

13. Spanish to English:

Find the English meaning for each of the Spanish words or phrases from this chapter.

Spanish	English
a) *claro*	
b) *catedral*	
c) *Feliz Navidad*	
d) *cuento de hadas*	
e) *atole de chocolate*	

Language Activities

1. Copy out any three sentences from this chapter and underline the **verbs**.

   _____
   _____
   _____

2. Beside each of the following words from this chapter, write its **root word**.

   a) kissed _____   b) propped _____

   c) carrying _____   d) rumbling _____

   e) worries _____   f) carefully _____

   g) occupied _____ h) hugged _____

Esperanza Rising
by Pam Muñoz Ryan

Chapter Ten

Los Aguacates - Avocados

Before you read the chapter:

Did you know that California grows 95 percent of the world's **avocados**? Californians put them into everything from ice cream to sushi. The English living in Jamaica called the avocado an "alligator pear". Investigate **three** additional facts about this interesting fruit. You may wish to include facts about its appearance, how it grows, and how it is beneficial to a person's diet.

_____
_____
_____
_____

Vocabulary:

1. **Antonyms** are words with opposite meanings. Draw a line from each word in column A to its antonym in column B.

Column A	Column B
taut	wealth
supple	permanent
susceptible	lax
squalor	protected
temporary	inflexible

Esperanza Rising
by Pam Muñoz Ryan

2. Use the words in column A to fill in the blanks in the sentences below.

   a) The strikers lived in _____.

   b) Mama was _____ to illnesses in her weakened condition.

   c) The drawstring was pulled _____.

   d) The young gymnast was very _____.

   e) Miguel's job with the railway was only _____.

Questions

Indicate whether the following statements are **True** or **False**.

_____ 1. Esperanza was saving her money to bring Abuelita to the camp to see Mama.

_____ 2. Esperanza soaked her hands in avocado pulp to cure a bad case of warts.

_____ 3. Mama's condition was complicated by a case of pneumonia.

_____ 4. Mama would not be able to receive visitors for at least six months.

_____ 5. To make her mother feel better, Esperanza did up her hair.

_____ 6. The main reason Esperanza shopped at the Japanese market was because it had the cheapest prices.

_____ 7. Esperanza was probably better educated than most American children of that time.

_____ 8. Esperanza bought a *piñata* for Pepe.

_____ 9. Marta had been tossed out of the migrant camp for refusing to work.

_____ 10. Marta told Esperanza that during the asparagus picking there would be a strike.

Esperanza Rising
by Pam Muñoz Ryan

Language Activities

1. Find **three** examples from this chapter of the following parts of speech.

Nouns	Verbs	Adjectives

2. **Interview** at least three other students for their views of this novel. (Try to get both positive and negative comments.) Write a brief **report** putting these views together.

_____
_____
_____
_____
_____
_____
_____
_____
_____

Esperanza Rising
by Pam Muñoz Ryan

Chapter Eleven

Los Espárragos - Asparagus

Before you read the chapter:

Defend or refute the following statement giving reasons for your opinion: "Something seemed very wrong about sending people away from their own 'free country' because they had spoken their minds."

_____
_____
_____
_____
_____

Vocabulary:

Analogies are equations in which the first pair of words has the same relationship as the second pair of words. For example, **stop** is to **go** as **fast** is to **slow**. In this example, both pairs of words are opposites. Choose the best word from the word box to complete each of the analogies below.

| insult | cautious | voluntary | delicate | anguish |
| cringe | desolate | freedom | despondent | clench |

1. **Tall** is to **short** as **slavery** is to _____.

2. **Beautiful** is to **lovely** as **forsaken** is to _____.

3. **Skilled** is to **talented** as **pain** is to _____.

4. **Calm** is to **turbulent** as **unconscious** is to _____.

5. **Valuable** is to **precious** as **sad** is to _____.

6. **Adventurous** is to _____ as **full** is to **empty**.

Esperanza Rising
by Pam Muñoz Ryan

7. **Recoil** is to _____ as **love** is to **adore**.

8. **Compliment** is to _____ as **efficient** is to **incompetent**.

9. **Unbreakable** is to _____ as **scenic** is to **grotesque**.

10. **Grip** is to _____ as **modern** is to **fashionable**.

Questions

1. Why did Esperanza worry about not having a job?
   _____
   _____

2. Why did the strikers say they had to strike?
   _____
   _____

3. What were two ways that the strikers tried to intimidate the workers?
   _____
   _____

4. What was the danger of many more people coming into the area?
   _____
   _____

5. What was a "sweep"?
   _____
   _____

6. What was a "voluntary deportation"?
   _____
   _____

Esperanza Rising
by Pam Muñoz Ryan

7. What did Esperanza find when she went looking for rubber bands? What did she do about it?

_____
_____

Language Activities

1. Pretend you are a newspaper editor for *The Los Angeles Times* back in the 1930s and you are writing an **editorial** describing the events surrounding the **sweep** described in this chapter. Write the editorial, not only describing the events that happened, but also stating **your opinion** about what transpired and the way you feel about it.

_____
_____
_____
_____
_____
_____
_____
_____
_____
_____
_____

2. Create and design a **poster** advertising a meeting to discuss a general strike. Pretend you are Marta designing such an advertisement. Be sure to include a couple of key issues, information about where and when the meeting will take place, as well as a relevant picture which will attract a person's interest.

Esperanza Rising
by Pam Muñoz Ryan

Chapter Twelve

Los Duraznos - Peaches

Before you read the chapter:

Esperanza delivers a very strong **opinion** to Miguel in this chapter: "Miguel, do you not understand? You are still a second-class citizen because you act like one, letting them take advantage of you like that. Why don't you go to your boss and confront him? Why don't you speak up for yourself and your talents?" Do you think Miguel is receiving good advice? Defend your answer.

_____
_____

Vocabulary:

Replace the words that are underlined in the sentences below with a word from the word list in the box. Remember to consider the context of the word in the sentences, as some words have several meanings.

| cleanser | hopeful | committed | spoil |
| penitent | lamentable | worsened | faced |

1. Isabel was very **dedicated** to being appointed Queen of the May. _____

2. He didn't mean to **frustrate** her well-laid plans. _____

3. The workers **confronted** the strikers. _____

4. Esperanza was afraid to send her **pitiful** savings. _____

5. She was **optimistic** that everything would turn out right. _____

6. They applied an **antiseptic** to the dirty sink. _____

7. Mama's health **relapsed** over the weekend. _____

8. Esperanza was **ashamed** of her behavior. _____

Esperanza Rising
by Pam Muñoz Ryan

Questions

1. Why did Isabel think that the teacher might choose her to be Queen of the May?

2. Who were usually chosen to be Queen of the May?

3. Why do you think Isabel hated the particular crop that was being harvested?

4. Where would the people from Oklahoma be staying? What extra facilities would they enjoy?

5. Describe how Miguel lost his job as a mechanic.

6. What advantage did Miguel see in living in the United States?

7. When Miguel disappeared, where did he tell his father he was going and why?

Esperanza Rising
by Pam Muñoz Ryan

8. Why did Isabel's teacher say she chose someone other than Isabel? Do you think this was the real reason? Explain.
   _____
   _____

9. What did Esperanza give Isabel to cheer her up? Where did Isabel take the gift?
   _____
   _____

10. What good news did Esperanza receive regarding Mama?
    _____
    _____

11. What disastrous discovery did Esperanza make at the end of this chapter?
    _____
    _____

Esperanza Rising
by Pam Muñoz Ryan

Language Activities

1. Try to reassemble the word parts listed below into ten compound words found in this chapter.

yard	tub	rail	vine	bed
honey	stand	suckle	out	berry
under	grown	wash	no	road
noon	thing	after	china	side

   _____   _____
   _____   _____
   _____   _____
   _____   _____
   _____   _____

2. This chapter ends with the statements, "It was empty. The money orders were gone." Ending a chapter this way is called a **cliffhanger**. How else might the author have revealed that the money orders were gone, in a *cliffhanger sort of way*.

Esperanza Rising
by Pam Muñoz Ryan

Chapter Thirteen

Las Uvas - Grapes

Before you read the chapter:

At the conclusion of the last chapter Esperanza discovered that her money orders had been stolen. **Who** do you think stole them? **Predict** what you think will be done with the money.

_____
_____
_____

What do you think is significant about the first and last chapters of the novel having the **same** title? What is important about both being entitled "*Las Uvas* - Grapes"?

_____
_____
_____

Vocabulary:

Think of **synonyms** for the following words. Use a thesaurus if necessary.

gracious - _____

emotions - _____

escorted - _____

infuriate - _____

anticipate - _____

skeptical - _____

cacophony - _____

demonstrate - _____

Esperanza Rising
by Pam Muñoz Ryan

Questions

1. Who did they think stole Esperanza's money?

2. What news of Miguel did Alfonso bring Esperanza one morning?

3. Whom did Miguel bring back with him?

4. Describe Mama's reaction upon seeing her mother.

5. What premonition did Abuelita have?

6. When Esperanza told a story to Abuelita, how did Esperanza measure time?

7. According to Esperanza, what will happen if you lie on the ground and stay very still?

Esperanza Rising
by Pam Muñoz Ryan

8. How do you think it was possible for Esperanza to hover high above the valley?
   _____
   _____

9. Describe your reaction to the novel's concluding sentence: "Do not ever be afraid to start over." What gave Esperanza the right to offer this advice to Isabel?
   _____
   _____

Language Activities

1. Create a **timeline** for *Esperanza Rising* indicating the **ten most important events** of the novel and the order in which they happened.

2. Create a **book cover** for *Esperanza Rising*. Be sure to include the title, author, and a picture that will make other students want to read the novel.

Answer Key

Chapter One - Las Uvas: (page 11)
Vocabulary:
1. anticipation
2. premonition
3. forlorn
4. tormented
5. philosophical
6. congregate
7. magnified
8. precisely
9. resentment
10. resurrected
11. distinguished
12. propriety

Questions:
1. grapes
2. El Rancho de las Rosas, Mexico - 1930
3. Marisol Rodríguez, Chita and Bertina
4. A revolution. He treated them very fairly and with kindness.
5. Crocheting. Esperanza suggested it took her mind off worry.
6. as a memorial to herself
7. The United States
8. They were from different social/economic classes.
9. Mayor. She thought he looked like an underfed billy goat.
10. Alfonso and Miguel
11. Her father was dead.
12. a) the housekeeper b) Esperanza's grandmother c) Esperanza's best friend
    d) Esperanza's mother e) Esperanza's father f) El jefe (the boss)
    g) Hortensia's son h) Papa's stepbrother

Language Activities:
Spanish Words - English Meaning: campesinos - field-workers; reina - queen; tío - uncle; la cosecha - harvest; El Rancho de las Rosas - Ranch of the Roses; Cuidate los dedos - Watch your fingers

Foreshadowing: "do not be afraid to start over" (p.15); Esperanza pricks her thumb on a thorn and thinks it will bring bad luck (p.8).

Chapter Two - Las Papayas: (page 16)
Vocabulary:

(Crossword answers: JOY, ANGUISH, PATIO, WISTFUL, PROPOSE, REALITY, AWKWARD, ATTENTIVE, ROSEHIP, SOLUTION, INTEND, CUSTOM)

Questions:
1. Her father was dead.
2. "Papa would have wanted it."
3. a doll
4. to take care of the family business
5. Answers may vary - she did not like her uncle.
6. The house was worth twenty times more than his offer.
7. That she marry him. She would bring Luis prestige. She had no respect for Luis.
8. the memories of the roses
9. Anza
10. that Luis intends to take over the ranch one way or the other

Chapter Three - Los Higos: *(page 20)*
Vocabulary:
1. <u>famished</u> - the other words all mean *large*
2. <u>delight</u> - the other words all mean *to cry out*
3. <u>purchase</u> - the other words all mean *to give*
4. <u>devotion</u> - the other words all mean *a choice*
5. <u>affluent</u> - the other words all mean *savage*
6. <u>persuaded</u> - the other words all mean *bitter*
7. <u>accidental</u> - the other words all mean *on purpose*

Questions:
home; Miguel; uncles; servants; proposal; grapes; poverty; influence; United States; Abuelita; nuns; visa; Luis; phoenix; ashes; convent; figs; sadness

Chapter Four - Las Guayabas: *(page 24)*
Vocabulary:
1. rebel
2. constant
3. spellbind
4. strange
5. delicate
6. rise and fall
7. suitcase
8. boring
9. reddish brown
10. familiar

Questions:
1. hidden in a wagon
2. a) when thieves robbed their house and they hid under the bed
   b) He released his mouse.
   c) a train ride
3. two days
4. The people were dirty-looking and appeared untrustworthy.
5. a) She wouldn't show her the doll.
   b) She made her a yarn doll.
6. Now she and Esperanza were also peasants.

Language Activities:
2. wagons, dresses, cacti, valises, children, bellies, complexions, eyebrows, railroads, babies
3. a) rat   b) lace doilies   c) thank you   d) you're welcome
   e) sweets   f) lever   g) good luck

Chapter Five - Los Melones: *(page 28)*
Vocabulary:
1. departed
2. motionless
3. appearance
4. irritated
5. thin
6. ill
7. tied
8. feeling
9. flowed
10. purposefully

Questions:
1. He treated her with more respect.
2. They were sent back to Mexico.
3. They were getting water for their package.
4. through letters with Miguel's family
5. There they had to live in a tent.
6. a) the earth's heartbeat   b) Answers may vary - she felt herself rising above the earth.
7. very disrespectfully
8. Answers may vary - they didn't want them banding together for higher wages or better housing.
9. strike

Language Activities:
2. officials, Oklahoma, package, papers, past, paws, piled, plants, private, property

Chapter Six - Las Cebollas: *(page 32)*
Vocabulary:

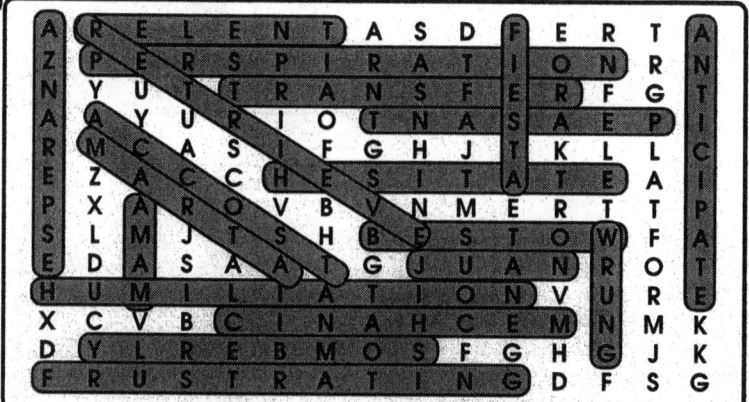

Questions:
1. The cabin was small and rough-looking.
2. to be together and miserable or to be together and happy
3. a) She felt her grandmother still had a lot of money and would come for them. b) Answers may vary.
4. looking after the babies
5. She let her hair down.
6. She was afraid that Silva would cry if she did.
7. Her husband used to work for Señor Rodríguez, their former neighbor.
8. Four of: plunged the diaper in water; scrubbed it with soap; scrubbed it on the washboard; wrung it out; transferred it to second tub; rinsed it; wrung it out again.
9. They had servants to do that sort of work.
10. Answers may vary - Esperanza used to have servants do all her work for her.

Language Activities:
2. a) Esperanza rode the train to Los Angeles.
   b) Señor Rodrígues enjoyed picking peaches, guavas, onions and plums in California.
   c) From Zacatecas, Isabel drove a wagon to San Francisco.

Chapter Seven - Las Almendras: *(page 36)*
Vocabulary: Answers may vary.

Questions:
1. She was only hurt emotionally, not physically.
2. a) grotto or shrine of rocks and roses around the base of a tub   b) Answers may vary.
3. Answers may vary - the memory of her father would always be with her.
4. There was a *jamaica* or party that evening.
5. You should just laugh.
6. a) strike   b) higher wages and better housing
7. They had to feed their families and there were no other jobs.
8. guilty

Chapter Eight - Las Ciruelas: *(page 40)*
Vocabulary:
1. reposition   2. atrocious   3. occasionally   4. preoccupied   5. frantic
6. peculiar   7. sympathetic   8. spasm   9. grim   10. infection

Questions:
1. She thought they might be ill.   2. rice water   3. the plums
4. She wandered away.   5. "To eat and feed our children."   6. a dust storm
7. The storm was too bad.   8. the dust storm
9. The cotton crop was buried in the sand.   10. The grapes are higher off the ground.
11. She was feverish and ill.   12. It is a disease of the lungs caused by dust spores.

Chapter Nine - Las Papas: *(page 44)*
Vocabulary:
1. agile   2. piercing   3. huge   4. pity   5. longed
6. fastened   7. cold   8. administrator

Questions:
1. They put up extra layers of newspaper and cardboard.   2. Abuelita's blanket
3. Abuelita   4. Answers may vary - it was a very trying time.
5. crocheting her grandmother's blanket   6. her depression
7. to pay the medical bills and to bring her grandmother to California
8. They would hire her for the next job.   9. They are planted.
10. People are sent back to Mexico.   11. more work; Mama to get well; soft hands
12. a small, smooth stone
13. a) certainly   b) church   c) Merry Christmas   d) fairytale   e) chocolate milk

Language Activities:
2. a) kiss   b) prop   c) carry   d) rumble   e) worry
   f) care   g) occupy   h) hug

Chapter Ten - Las Aguacates: *(page 48)*
Vocabulary:
1. taut - lax; supple - inflexible; susceptible - protected; squalor - wealth; temporary - permanent
2. a) squalor   b) susceptible   c) taut   d) supple   e) temporary

Questions:
1. T   2. F   3. T   4. F   5. T   6. F   7. T   8. F   9. T   10. T

Chapter Eleven - Los Espárragos: *(page 51)*
Vocabulary:
1. freedom   2. desolate   3. anguish   4. voluntary   5. despondent
6. cautious   7. cringe   8. insult   9. delicate   10. clench

Questions:
1. Her mother needed medicine.
2. They couldn't feed their children.
3. Two of: put snakes in crate; shards of glass in bins; shouts; threatening
4. They might lose their jobs.
5. The police rounded up the strikers.
6. People chose to go back to Mexico with a family member who was being deported.
7. She found Marta. She hid her and gave her an apron to wear when she left.

Chapter Twelve - Los Duraznos: *(page 54)*
Vocabulary:
1. committed   2. spoil   3. faced   4. lamentable
5. hopeful   6. cleanser   7. worsened   8. penitent

Questions:
1. She had the best marks in the class.
2. white children
3. She probably got very tired of the crop they were picking.
4. In an old army barracks. They would have inside toilets, hot water and a swimming pool.
5. A group of men from Oklahoma said they would do his job for half the money.
6. In the United States he had a small chance to become more than what he was in Mexico.
7. to northern California to look for work on the railroad
8. Answers may vary - the choice was made on more than just grades
9. Her doll. She took the doll to school.
10. Mama would leave the hospital in a week.
11. Her money orders were gone.

Language Activities:
honeysuckle, railroad, understand, afternoon, washtub, outgrown, nothing, vineyard, chinaberry, bedside

Chapter Thirteen - Las Uvas: *(page 58)*
Vocabulary: Answers may vary.

Questions:
1. Miguel
2. They were to meet him at the bus station at three o'clock.
3. Abuelita
4. She was overjoyed.
5. She felt that something was wrong with Mama.
6. in spans of fruits and vegetables
7. You will feel the earth's heart beating.
8. Answers may vary.
9. Answers may vary - Esperanza had started her life over in the United States.

www.ingramcontent.com/pod-product-compliance
Lightning Source LLC
Chambersburg PA
CBHW050351100426
42734CB00041B/3142